SACRED
RHYTHMS
PARTICIPANT'S GUIDE

ALSO BY RUTH HALEY BARTON

An Ordinary Day with Jesus

Invitation to Solitude and Silence

Longing for More

Sacred Rhythms

Strengthening the Soul of Your Leadership

RUTH HALEY BARTON

SACRED RHYTHMS

SIX SESSIONS

*Spiritual Practices that Nourish Your Soul
and Transform Your Life*

PARTICIPANT'S GUIDE

ZONDERVAN®

ZONDERVAN.com/
AUTHORTRACKER
follow your favorite authors

ZONDERVAN

Sacred Rhythms Participant's Guide
Copyright © 2011 by Ruth Haley Barton

Requests for information should be addressed to:

Zondervan, *Grand Rapids, Michigan 49530*

ISBN 978-0-310-32881-0

Cover design: Tammy Johnson
Interior design: Tina Henderson

Printed in the United States of America

11 12 13 14 15 /DCI/ 26 25 24 23 22 21 20 19 18 17 16 15 14 13 12 11 10 9 8 7 6 5 4 3 2 1

We long to see our lives whole and to know that they matter. We wonder whether our many activities might ever come together in a way of life that is good for ourselves and others. Does all this activity make a difference beyond ourselves? Are we really living in right relationship to other people, to the created world and to God?... We yearn for a deeper understanding of how to order human life in accord with what is true and good.

CRAIG DYKSTRA AND DOROTHY BASS,
PRACTICING OUR FAITH

Contents

Welcome to Sacred Rhythms

Sacred Rhythms is a curriculum designed to help you arrange your life around a regular pattern of spiritual practices that God can use to nourish your soul and transform your life.

The idea of sacred rhythms is rooted in the ancient Christian practice of a *rule of life*—a practice that originated with great spiritual teachers like St. Augustine, St. Benedict, and Teresa of Avila as they provided spiritual guidance for the monks and nuns living under their care. Of course, our lives today are very different from those living in religious orders, but the practice of ordering our lives in such a way that God has access to our souls and freedom to do his transforming work in us has great power for us today.

To begin, we will explore our need to pay attention to our God-given desires, so that we know what we want to arrange our lives *for*. Then we will experience key spiritual disciplines, so that you can eventually put together a rhythm that works for *you*. Each session includes teaching and discussion about a particular spiritual discipline or practice and then a guided experience with that practice. Some of the guided experiences might feel different from anything you have done before, and you may even feel a little awkward at first. That's okay. I encourage you to at least try each discipline to see if it does indeed open up space for God. Your participant's guide will provide helpful instruction for continuing to explore and practice the discipline during the week, and you are also encouraged to read the corresponding chapters in *Sacred Rhythms* (the book on which this curriculum is based) for further information and support.

The disciplines you will experience here are ones that spiritual seekers down through the centuries have practiced as a way of opening to

the transforming presence of God. I am glad you have chosen to deepen
your spiritual journey in this way and I pray God's blessing upon you.

— RUTH HALEY BARTON

OF NOTE

This curriculum is based on *Sacred Rhythms: Arranging Our
Lives for Spiritual Transformation* by Ruth Haley Barton (Inter-
Varsity Press, 2006).

Unless otherwise noted, the quotations interspersed
throughout this participant's guide are excerpts from the
book, used by permission.

Before You Get Started...
Guidelines for Spiritual Friends

Your small group provides spiritual companionship for you as you explore the spiritual disciplines that help you to seek God. Spiritual friends listen to one another's desire for God, nurture that desire in each other, and support one another as each group member seeks to live in a way that is consistent with his or her desire for God. Spiritual friendships are not the place for giving advice, solving problems, and fixing people. They are not even *primarily* about Bible study — although significant interaction with the Scriptures will be offered in every session. Instead, your small group is a circle of friends that can assist you in paying attention to the ways God is moving in your life as you practice the disciplines. Good small groups will support one another in responding faithfully to God's presence. This commitment to community and spiritual friendship is in itself a powerful practice that is very important in the spiritual life.

Here are some simple guidelines you can commit yourselves to, guidelines that will help you to be effective spiritual companions for one another:

- *We will* make every effort to try each of the spiritual practices as they are presented.
- *We will* support and pray for one another as we practice the disciplines.
- *We will* create and maintain a safe environment for strong emotions, tough questions, and genuine curiosity. This means we

will listen rather than fix, ask questions rather than give answers or advice, and keep the focus on transformation rather than information.

- *We will* seek to be appropriately self-disclosing in the group, but we will never force or coerce anyone to share.
- *We will* pay particular attention to the times and ways in which God is moving in each person's life and seek to affirm evidence of each person's growth and transformation.
- *We will* honor confidentiality. What is shared in the group stays in the group!

It is important to take time at the beginning of your first meeting to go over these guidelines and agree to them together. It might even be helpful for group members to sign the bottom of this page as an indication that they have read and agree to companion one another in this way.

Starting with your second meeting, begin each session with a few moments of sharing how your practice of the previous discipline went.

Desire: Longing for More in the Spiritual Life

The reason we do not see God is the faintness of our desire.

— MEISTER ECKHART

DESIRE. The spiritual life begins with the willingness to name our desire in Jesus' presence. Your desire for God and your capacity to reach for more of God than you have right now is the deepest essence of who you are. It is one of the most powerful motivators for a life lived with intentionality and focus.

"YOU MIGHT THINK THAT *your woundedness or your sinfulness is the truest thing about you. You might think that your giftedness or your personality type or your job title or your identity as husband or wife, mother or father, somehow defines you. But in reality, it is your desire for God and your capacity to reach for God that is the deepest essence of who you are.*"

LEARN ABOUT IT
Video #1: Longing for More (14 minutes)

Following the curriculum introduction, watch the teaching segment for session one and use the following outline to record anything that stands out to you.

When was the last time you felt yourself longing for a deeper level of spiritual transformation?

spiritual desires — name the desire.

get Jesus' attention
humble ourselves.

Jesus asked people: What is it you want? What do you seek? What do you want me to do for you?

The story of Bartimaeus (Mark 10:46–52)
- Crying out from the place of our deep need: "Lord, Jesus Christ, son of David, have mercy on me, a sinner."

- Leaving behind our cloak

- Naming our desire in Jesus' presence: "My teacher, I want to see."

- Following Jesus in a new way

"THE SPIRITUAL LIFE BEGINS *with the longing that stirs way down deep, underneath the noise, the activity, the drivenness of our lives.... The stirring of spiritual desire indicates that God's Spirit is already at work within us, drawing us to himself.*"

Group Discussion

1. Describe a time when you were aware of your own desire or desperation for God to do something in your life.

   Change our mindsets

   He first loved us.

   a free gift.

2. What is the desire you are most aware of in your life right now?

3. What part of the Bartimaeus story do you relate to most strongly or even resist most strongly relative to the desire you are naming?

EXPERIENCE IT
Video #2: Finding Ourselves in the Story (9 minutes)

The "Experience It" segment provides an opportunity for you to engage in a guided experience of paying attention to your desire. Ruth Haley Barton will give specific directions in the video, so it's not necessary to follow along in your participant's guide. In fact, it is a good idea to close your book so it does not distract you. The notes below are provided as a resource and reference as you continue to practice this discipline on your own after the session.

* * *

This is a guided meditation based on the story of Bartimaeus in Mark 10:46–52. It is an invitation to find yourself in the story and allow the words of Jesus to speak to you personally.

- Find a comfortable position that allows you to remain alert.
- Place your hands open on your lap, close your eyes, and breathe deeply.
- Imagine yourself in the story of Bartimaeus ...
  Sitting on the dusty road ...
  Calling out to Jesus from the noisy crowd ...
  Hearing voices trying to silence you ...
  Being called by Jesus ...
  Throwing off your cloak and running to Jesus ...
  What words do you cry out? Who tries to silence you? What do you need to throw off in order to come to Jesus?

Hearing Jesus ask you, "What do you want me to do for you?"
What do you say in response?

Hearing Jesus' response to your request
What does Jesus say to you in response to your desire?

To practice the disciplines.

- If you haven't been able to name your desire, just stay with Jesus in that place and listen to what he has to say to you. If you have trouble getting in touch with your desire, it might help to begin with the statement "What I most need/want from you right now is ..." and then let your thoughts flow.

OPTIONAL ACTIVITY
If you have additional time or are using this study in a retreat setting, spend some time alone at this point (a half hour is good). Journal or take a walk or find a quiet place to be in God's presence and listen and respond to the question "What do I most need/want from you right now?"

Group Discussion

1. How does it feel to be asked and invited to pay attention to your desire?

2. Where do you find yourself in the story of Bartimaeus? In the crowd? Sitting by the side of the road? Able to cry out (or unwilling to cry out) to Jesus? Running to Jesus (with or without your cloak)?

3. Are you able to hear Jesus asking you the question "What do you want me to do for you?" What is your response to him?

"WHEN YOU GO TO *pray, do not try to express yourself in fancy words, for often it is the simple repetitious phrases of a little child that our Father in heaven finds most irresistible. . . . When you find a satisfaction in a certain word of your prayer, stop at that point.*"

— JOHN CLIMACUS

Closing Prayer

Close your time with prayer. Ask God to:

- Help you identify and name your desires
- Give you a greater sensitivity to the work of the Holy Spirit in your life, refining and clarifying your desire
- Help you become faithful companions to one another in your group as you practice these disciplines together

BETWEEN SESSIONS

Breath Prayer

Once you begin to uncover your true desire for God, you can practice a very simple discipline called a *breath prayer*. Breath prayer does not come primarily from the mind, which is where most of our words come from. Instead, the breath prayer arises from the depth of our desire and need, just like Bartimaeus' prayer: "Lord Jesus Christ, son of David, have mercy on me!" In fact, you could also call it a "gut prayer" because it comes from such a deep "gut" level within us.

The breath prayer requires no thought to remember — once we really know it! It is typically a short (only six to eight syllables) expression that we pray rhythmically with the inhalation and exhalation of our breathing. Breath prayer is powerful because it is an expression of our heart's deepest yearning coupled with a name for God that is meaningful and intimate for us.

Between now and the next session, take some time to quietly explore the desire that is stirring in your own heart. What does it feel like? What words begin to express it? When do you experience it most strongly? Then use the following exercise to discover your own breath prayer.

- Return to the Bartimaeus story and imagine Jesus calling you by name and asking, "_____, what do you want?" Allow your truest answer to come up from deep within you and express it to God. The following phrase might help you to begin.

  God, what I most want from you right now is . . .

- Choose your favorite name or image for God. For example, you could use one of the following names: God, Jesus, Father, Creator, Spirit, Breath of Life, Lord, Shepherd, Holy One, etc. Choose a name that best expresses who God is for you right now in your relationship or expresses who you need or want him to be.

  A name for God that is most meaningful for me right now is . . .

- Now combine your name for God with the expression of your heart's desire. You may also be drawn to a phrase from Scripture or a prayer from Christian tradition that seems to capture your desire at this time; for example, "Come, Holy Spirit," "Lord Jesus Christ, have mercy on me," or "My Teacher, let me see again." There is no right or wrong way to put these two together.

- Express your prayer in a way that is easy to speak in the steady rhythm of your breathing. There may be various ways of saying your prayer, and you may want to write them down until you have a prayer of about six to eight syllables.
- Once you have discovered your breath prayer, pray it into the spaces of your day—when you are waiting, when you are worried or anxious, when you need a sense of God's presence. Over time you will learn to pray it underneath all the other thoughts and words that swirl around you throughout the day, and eventually you will discover that you are praying without ceasing (1 Thessalonians 5:17) in a way that has deep meaning and great power.

For Further Reading

For further information and guidance regarding the dynamic of desire and the practice of breath prayer as we have explored it in this session, read chapters 1 and 4 of *Sacred Rhythms* by Ruth Haley Barton.

Reflect and Journal

In preparation for the next session, take some time to reflect on your experience with paying attention to desire and seeking to discover your own breath prayer. It may help you to write about it in your journal or use the journal pages provided here. Consider these questions as you write:

- Where are you in the process of naming your desire in Jesus' presence and discovering your breath prayer?
- What has it been like to walk through this week more aware of your desire?
- If you have discovered your breath prayer, how/when have you used it? What was that like?

JOURNAL

JOURNAL

Solitude and Silence: Creating Space for God

Without solitude it is virtually impossible to have a spiritual life.

— HENRI NOUWEN

SOLITUDE is that time when we pull away from our life in the company of others in order to give our full and undivided attention to God. Silence deepens the experience of solitude. In silence we withdraw not only from outer noise but also from the "inner noise" of our thoughts, human strivings, intellectual hard work, and inner compulsions so that we can listen to God.

"THE LONGING FOR SOLITUDE *is the longing for God. It is the longing to experience union with God unmediated by the ways we typically try to relate to God.... It is the practice that spiritual seekers down through the ages have used to experience intimacy with God rather than just talking about it.*"

LEARN ABOUT IT
Video #1: Creating Space for God (12 minutes)

As you watch the teaching segment for session two, use the following outline to record anything that stands out to you.

Solitude is the most basic spiritual discipline.

Silence = Letting go of our *inner* distractions
Solitude = Letting go of our *outer* distractions

Elijah in 1 Kings 19:1–19

In solitude, we start by saying something *true* to God.

We also learn how to let go. We give up control.

We create space for God.

We learn how to rest in God—even with the things that are troubling us.

We let go of distractions

We allow ourselves full self-disclosure: the good, the bad, and the ugly.
• Recognize aspects of ourselves and our lives that are *good* and going well.

• Acknowledge aspects of our lives that are going *badly.*

• Speak the truth about aspects of ourselves and our lives that are *ugly.*

Eventually, the chaos does settle—just like a jar of river water that has sat long enough for the sediment to settle and the water to become clear.

7/5
get your rest
The culture that we are living

"MOST OF US ARE *more tired than we know at the soul level. We are teetering on the brink of dangerous exhaustion, and we really cannot do anything else until we have gotten some rest.... Before it can be anything else, solitude needs to be a place of rest in God.***"**

Group Discussion
1. Ruth uses words and phrases like *desperation, things that needed fixing in my life, longings that were painfully unmet, performance-oriented drivenness, Christian fatigue syndrome,* and *desire for a way of life that works* to describe the state of her life as she was first being invited into solitude and silence. What parts of her description do you most relate to, and why?

We are in God's presence—
There were no words

How do you respond to the image of "the jar of river water all shaken up"? Does this reflect your life right now? Why or why not?

2. As you listened to the descriptions of solitude and silence, did you feel drawn to them or were you resistant to them? What do you find appealing about the idea of solitude? What hesitations or fears, if any, do you feel about spending time in solitude?

3. What part of Elijah's story did you relate to most strongly? What do you sense God saying to you through this story?

You can't pray for "A"
but do the study for "C"

EXPERIENCE IT
Video #2: The Discipline of Silence (16 minutes)

The "Experience It" segment provides an opportunity for you to engage in a guided experience of solitude and silence. Ruth Haley Barton will read a prayer, with a portion of time afterward allotted for silent reflection. It's not necessary to follow along in your participant's guide. In fact, it is a good idea to close your book so it does not distract you. The notes below are provided as a resource and reference as you continue to practice this discipline on your own after the session.

* * *

When we engage in the disciplines of solitude and silence, we let go of our usual distractions so that we can be present to the One who is always present with us. We are willing to be with God just as we are—awake, alert, and receptive to whatever he wants to say to us. If this is a new practice for you, you might want to begin your time in solitude by borrowing the opening line from the prayer Ruth read in the video presentation—"Holy One, there is something I wanted to tell you ..."—and just seeing what comes. You might be surprised at what your soul wants to say to God ... and what God wants to say to your soul. (A fuller version of this prayer, "There Is Something I Wanted to Tell You," by Ted Loder, is included as Appendix B, page 85.)

> **OPTIONAL ACTIVITY**
> If you have additional time or if you are using this study in a retreat setting, spend another thirty to sixty minutes in silence (journal if you like). You might want to sit with the idea "Holy One, there is something I wanted to tell you ..." and then see what comes. (See Appendix B, page 85.) When your time of silence is over, come back together for the group discussion.

Group Discussion

1. What was it like for you to sit quietly, to rest in God, and allow your soul to come out? Refreshing? Challenging? Confusing? Peaceful?

what's the invitation to me heart &

invitation

2. What did your soul need to say to God? What (if anything) did God say to your soul?

3. Did this experience raise any questions or feelings of resistance for you? If so, name them.

4. What are your thoughts/feelings about incorporating solitude into your life more regularly?

"SILENCE DEEPENS OUR EXPERIENCE *of solitude, because in silence we choose to unplug not only from the constant stimulation of life in the company of others but also from our own addiction to noise, words, and activity. It creates a space for listening to the knowings that go beyond words.... The most essential question in solitude is: How have I been wanting to be with God, and how has God been wanting to be with me?*"

Closing Prayer

Take time as a group to pray in some of the following directions:

- Thank God for his presence with you during the time of solitude and silence.
- Pray for the courage to continue to speak honestly with God and follow whatever invitations come from your times with him.
- Pray for wisdom about how to set aside time for solitude and silence between sessions and for the discipline to keep it.

"SOLITUDE EVENTUALLY OFFERS A *quiet gift of grace, a gift that comes whenever we are able to face ourselves honestly: the gift of acceptance, of compassion, for who we are as we are. As we allow ourselves to be known in solitude, we discover we are known by love. Beyond the pain of self-discovery there is a love that does not condemn us but calls us to itself. This love receives us as we are.*"

— PARKER PALMER, *TO KNOW AS WE ARE KNOWN*

BETWEEN SESSIONS
Practicing Solitude and Silence

- During the next week, set aside ten, fifteen, or twenty minutes a day for solitude at a time that works for you. It could be morning, over your lunch hour, during quiet moments after dinner or before you go to bed, or you might choose a more extended time on the weekend. Be realistic regarding the time you choose based on what's going on in your family and in your life at work.

- The goal of this week's practice is for you to learn to begin your times in solitude by being quiet and letting your soul come out and rest in God's presence. You might want to use your breath prayer as the prayer that helps you enter into your time of silence. If you get distracted, pray your breath prayer as a way of bringing you back to your desire and intention to be present with God.

- Find a spot where you can be quiet and alone. Settle into a comfortable position in your body and sit quietly for a few moments, breathing deeply, becoming aware of God's presence with you and your desire to be present with God.

- Begin to notice what is true about your life. Don't rush this or force it. Let your soul venture out and say something to you that perhaps you have had a hard time acknowledging. If you are having a hard time getting started, the following questions are a helpful way to begin:

  Is there a particular joy you are celebrating?

  A loss you are grieving?

  Are there tears that have been waiting to be shed?

  A question that is stirring?

  Anger, frustration, or some other thought or emotion that you need to express to God but just haven't had the opportunity?

- Sit with what comes into your awareness, becoming conscious of God's presence with you in whatever you are aware of. Don't try to do anything except experience it. Don't scare it away. Feel the difference between trying to *fix* it and just *being with* it. Feel the difference between *doing* something with it and *resting* with it. Feel the difference between trying to fight it and letting God fight for you.

- What does it mean for you to *be still and let God act for you* in this particular area? What are you able to know in the stillness that you have not been able to know in the noise and busyness of your life?
- After you spend time in silence, you may also want to use this time to journal your thoughts as prayers to God or record what you feel God is saying to you using the journal pages provided.

For Further Reading

As you reflect further on what you have learned in this session and begin practicing solitude and silence, read chapter 2 of *Sacred Rhythms.* If you find that you would like even more guidance and support for your practice, you might also want to read *Invitation to Solitude and Silence: Experiencing God's Transforming Presence*, also by Ruth Haley Barton.

Reflect and Journal

Use your own journal or these journal pages to say something honest to God.

Holy One, there is something I want to tell you ...

JOURNAL

JOURNAL

Lectio Divina:
Encountering God in Scripture

"Is not my word like fire?" declares the Lord, "and like a hammer that shatters a rock?"

— JEREMIAH 23:29

LECTIO DIVINA, a Latin phrase pronounced lex-ee-oh di-veen-ah and translated *divine* or *sacred reading*, is an approach to Scripture that opens us to a life-transforming encounter with God within the biblical text. It refers to an ancient practice of the early mothers and fathers of the Christian faith, and it is a slower and more reflective reading of the Scriptures that allows God to address us directly, according to what he knows we need.

"WHEN WE ENGAGE THE *Scriptures for spiritual transformation, we engage not only our mind but also our heart, our emotions, our body, our curiosity, our imagination, and our will. We open ourselves to a deeper level of understanding and insight that grows out of and leads us deeper into our personal relationship with the One behind the text. It is in the context of relational intimacy that real life change takes place.*"

LEARN ABOUT IT
Video #1: Reading for Transformation (11 minutes)

As you watch the teaching segment for session three, use the following outline to record anything that stands out to you.

Reading Scripture as a love letter: Are you reading for information or for transformation?

Approaching the Scriptures to hear God speak to you (1 Samuel 3:10)

Lectio divina—divine or sacred reading

The four moves of *lectio divina*
1. READ (*lectio*): Listen for the word or the phrase that is addressed to you.

2. REFLECT (*meditatio*): How is my life touched by this word today?

3. RESPOND (*oratio*): What is my response to God based on what I have read and encountered?

4. REST (*contemplatio*): Simply rest in the Word of God.

"LECTIO DIVINA REMINDS ME *of how the desert fathers read Scripture. For them, contact with Scripture was 'contact with fire that burns, disturbs, calls violently to conversion.' The story is told of someone coming to Abba Pambo, asking him to teach him a psalm. Pambo begins teaching him Psalm 38, but hardly has he pronounced the first verse, 'I will be watchful of my ways, for fear I should sin with my tongue,' when the brother said he did not wish to hear anymore. He tells Pambo, 'This verse is enough for me; please God, may I have the strength to learn it and put it into practice.' Nineteen years later he was still trying.*"

Group Discussion

1. How would you describe your typical interaction with Scripture? Do you find yourself approaching the Bible like a newspaper or a textbook, or is it more like reading a love letter?

2. How does the way you read something affect what you receive from it or how it impacts you? Give an example of something you have read recently that led to a change in your life. What led to this transformation?

3. Hebrews 4:12 states that Scripture is alive and active and sharper than any two-edged sword. What does that mean to you? How might this image encourage you as you interact with Scripture?

EXPERIENCE IT
Video #2: Lectio Divina (12 minutes)

The "Experience It" segment provides an opportunity for you to engage in a guided experience of sacred reading. Ruth Haley Barton will give specific directions in the video, so it's not necessary to follow along in your participant's guide. In fact, it is a good idea to close your book so it does not distract you. The notes below are provided as a resource and reference as you continue to practice this discipline on your own after the session.

* * *

The practice of *lectio divina* is rooted in the belief that through the presence of the Holy Spirit the Scriptures are alive, active, and God-breathed.

This was true when they were first inspired and written, and it is true today when we engage them for spiritual transformation (Hebrews 4:12).

- Take a moment to become quiet. You may want to close your eyes as a way of eliminating distraction and focusing inward. Let your body relax and allow yourself to become consciously aware of God's presence with you.
- Sit with both feet on the floor, back straight but not stiff or uncomfortable, hands placed comfortably on your lap.
- Express your willingness to hear from God in these moments by using a brief prayer such as "Come, Lord Jesus" or "Here I am" or "Speak, Lord, for your servant is listening."
- Listen to the words of Isaiah 43:1–4 as they are read aloud to you. Each time the Scripture is read, you are encouraged to listen in a slightly different way to the reading:

  First Reading—Listen for the word or phrase that catches your attention. Then just savor the word.

  Second Reading—Listen for the way in which this passage connects with your life today.

  Third Reading—Listen for an invitation from God contained in his word to you. Respond honestly to God about what you are hearing—a response that flows out of your deepest longings and desire for God.

  Fourth Reading—Rest in the word God has given you, knowing that he who has called you will be faithful to bring it to pass (1 Thessalonians 5:24).

- The culmination of the practice of *lectio divina* is "resolve." Stay with the word that God has given to you. Commit to carry it with you into your everyday life and continue to discover what it means for you to live it out.

"WHEN OUR RESPONSE HAS *been played out in all of its fury, angst, or exuberance, we come to a place of rest in God. Here there are no expectations, demands, no need to know, no desire but to be in the Divine Presence, receptive to what God desires to do with us.*"

— MARJORIE THOMPSON, *SOULFEAST*

OPTIONAL ACTIVITY

If you have additional time or are using this study in a retreat setting, now would be a good occasion to create some space for personal solitude. Reflect further on your conversation with God: what you have heard, what you feel God's invitation is to you, and how you are responding. Journaling is an excellent follow-up to an experience with *lectio divina* since powerful things take place in this process and we are not always ready to talk about them right away. An additional fifteen or twenty minutes of time alone can be very helpful for each group member.

Group Discussion

1. How was the *lectio* process the same and/or different from the way you normally read Scripture?

2. What move(s) in the *lectio divina* was most helpful or meaningful? Which move was most challenging?

3. What was God's invitation to you through this reading? How might you practice the final move of *lectio divina*, the resolve to live out the word that has been given to you?

Closing Prayer

Take time as a group to pray in some of the following directions:

- Thank God for speaking to you through his Word.
- Pray for the courage and resolve to live out the specific word you have received.
- Express your desire for God to continue to speak to you through his Word this week.

BETWEEN SESSIONS
Practicing Lectio Divina

Between sessions, practice incorporating *lectio divina* into the time you have been setting aside for solitude and silence. Consider using one or more of the passages below to get started, or if you are already using a reading schedule to study the Scriptures, use the *lectio* process with a passage from your reading. Or you might want to use the *lectio* process with the passage your pastor preached from most recently. Be sure to select no more than four to six verses, unless it's a story, which can be a little longer. You can also read through a book of the Bible or an entire chapter in bite-size portions as demonstrated by the passages from John and Colossians.

Suggested Scriptures: Psalm 23; Psalm 27:1–5; Psalm 63:1–4; Isaiah 43:1–4; Isaiah 55:6–9; Matthew 14:22–32; Luke 10:38–41; John 10:1–6, 7–10, 11–18; John 12:1–8; Ephesians 3:14–19; Colossians 3:1–4, 5–11, 12–17.

The practice of *lectio divina* includes a time of preparation, reading the same short passage of Scripture four times, and then taking that word with us into our everyday lives with a resolve to live it out in concrete ways.

- **PREPARE (*silencio*).** Take a moment to become quiet. You may want to close your eyes as a way of eliminating distraction and focusing inward. Let your body relax and allow yourself to become consciously aware of God's presence with you.
- **READ (*lectio*).** Turn to the passage and begin to read slowly, pausing between phrases and sentences. You may read silently to yourself or you might find it helpful to read the passage aloud and allow the words to echo and settle into your heart. As you read, listen for the word or phrase that strikes you or catches your attention. Allow for a moment of silence, then repeat that word or phrase softly to yourself, pondering it and savoring it as though pondering the words of a loved one. This is the word that is meant for you. Be content to listen simply and openly, without judging or analyzing.
- **REFLECT (*meditatio*).** Once you have heard the "word" that is

meant for you, read the passage again and listen for the way in which this passage connects with your life. Ask, "What is it in my life right now that needs to hear this word?" After reading, allow several moments of silence to explore thoughts, perceptions, and sensory impressions. If the passage is a story, perhaps ask yourself, "Where am I in this scene? What do I hear as I imagine myself in the story or hear these words addressed specifically to me? How does this story connect with my own life experience?"

- **RESPOND (*oratio*).** Read the passage once again, and listen for your own response. In the moments of silence that follow this reading, allow a prayer to flow spontaneously from your heart. At this point you are entering into a personal dialogue with God. You might also listen to see if God is inviting you to act or respond in some way to the word you have heard. You might find it helpful to write your prayers or to journal at this point.

- **REST (*contemplatio*).** In this final reading you are invited to return to a place of rest in God. You have given your response, and now you move into a time of waiting and resting in God's presence. This is a posture of being yielded and open to God.

- **RESOLVE (*incarnatio*).** The culmination of the *lectio* process is resolving to live out the word that you have received from God, committing to carry this word with you each day and to live it out in the context of daily life and activity. As you continue to listen to the word throughout the day, God will lead you into new ways of understanding what it means to have the word "live" in you. You may even want to select an image or a picture or a symbol that you can carry around with you as a constant reminder of the word that was given to you.

For Further Reading

As you reflect on your experience of *lectio divina* and begin practicing it on your own, read chapter 3 of *Sacred Rhythms*.

Reflect and Journal

Journaling is an excellent complement to the practice of *lectio divina*. You can start your journal entry by writing, "God, what I hear you saying to me is ..." and then record what you felt God saying to you during the *lectio* reading. You can also write down your response and watch as a conversation—a dialogue between you and God—begins to unfold.

In preparation for your next group meeting, you might also want to reflect on your encounters with God in Scripture throughout the week. How has the practice of *lectio* affected your relationship with God? What kinds of things are you hearing from God? How are you responding?

> **"**THE WORD OF SCRIPTURE *should never stop sounding in your ears and working in you all day long, just like the words of someone you love.... Do not ask 'How shall I pass this on?' but 'What does it say to me?' Then ponder this word long in your heart until it has gone right into you and taken possession of you.***"**
>
> —DIETRICH BONHOEFFER, *LIFE TOGETHER*

JOURNAL

JOURNAL

Honoring the Body: Flesh-and-Blood Spirituality

It is through our bodies that we participate in God's activity in the world.

— STEPHANIE PAULSELL, *PRACTICING OUR FAITH*

HONORING THE BODY is a practice that teaches us how to glorify God in our bodies and how to experience our bodies as the temple of the Holy Spirit. As we learn to honor the body and care for it as the temple of the Holy Spirit—a place of prayer and encounter with God—we are able to celebrate God's many good gifts to us in the body.

"WE ARE IN NEED *of a sacramental approach to life, in which the body is understood to be sacred because it is the place where God's Spirit has chosen to dwell. Given this, all aspects of life in the body can become places where we meet and know God in unique ways.*"

LEARN ABOUT IT
Video #1: Flesh-and-Blood Spirituality (8 minutes)

As you watch the teaching segment for session four, use the following outline to record anything that stands out to you.

An ambiguous legacy

Scripture affirms the significance of our bodies
- Genesis 1

- Psalm 139

- 1 Corinthians 6:19–20

Honoring the body as a spiritual practice involves
- Caring for the body

- Listening to the body

- Praying in the body

"SETTLING INTO A RELAXED *and comfortable position, letting go, and allowing the chair to fully support your body, breathing deeply as a way of releasing tension ... all of these can be very tangible ways of telling God that we are bringing our whole selves into his presence—body, mind, and soul.*"

Group Discussion

1. What life experiences have influenced the way you feel about your body, both positively and negatively?

2. What has been your experience of honoring or glorifying God in your body—in the way you care for your body, in corporate worship, in serving others? (See 1 Corinthians 6:19.) What are the dangers of *not* thinking of our bodies as a gift from God?

3. This session's teaching video mentioned many Scriptures and biblical themes that reflect the spiritual significance of our bodies. Which ones have influenced your own thinking about the body or struck you in a fresh way as you heard Ruth teach?

EXPERIENCE IT
Video #2: Honoring the Body (15 minutes)

The "Experience It" segment provides an opportunity for you to engage in a guided experience of honoring your body. Ruth Haley Barton will give specific directions in the video, so it's not necessary to follow along in your participant's guide. In fact, it is a good idea to close your book so it does not distract you. The notes below are provided as a resource and reference as you continue to practice this discipline on your own after the session.

* * *

Paying attention to your breathing is one of the simplest ways of getting in touch with your existence as a body. Our guided experience this session will begin with simply paying attention to our breathing.

- **Breathe.** Settle into a comfortable position, either in a chair or on the floor, and pay attention to your breathing. If your breathing is shallow, take time to breathe deeply.
- **Notice your body.** Gently turn your attention to your body and invite God to speak to you through your body. Notice how you feel right now about your body. Are you tense? Embarrassed? Do you have a sense of joy and well-being? Do you feel comfortable in your own body? If not, why?
- **Care about your body.** What is the condition of your body these days? Have you been caring for it consistently—eating right, sleeping enough, exercising regularly, attending to medical issues and concerns—or have you been ignoring it or even abusing it in some way?
- **Listen to your body.** Is there anything your body is trying to tell you? Any place of tension or discomfort that you have been ignoring? Any medical issues that require attention? Are there feelings of dis-ease that are vaguely unsettling? Listen to see if there is anything you have been keeping outside your conscious awareness.
- **Pray in your body.** Ruth will guide you in a simple prayer that involves three movements:
    Movement #1: Hold your hands open, in your lap.

Movement #2: Lift your hands slightly and hold your prayer in God's presence.

Movement #3: Raise your hands and move them apart to release your prayer to God.

Pray through each of these three movements, focusing on your family, your work, and yourself.

"I WILL PRAISE YOU *for I am fearfully and wonderfully made. Wonderful are your works, that I know very well.***"**

PSALM 139:14

OPTIONAL ACTIVITY
If you have more time or are using this study in a retreat setting, now is a good occasion to spend alone with God for additional reflection and journaling. Talk to God about your body, reflecting on how you are caring for or not caring for it. You may want to simply use this pause to rest (lie down, take a nap if you're on retreat, sit quietly in a chair or in the sun, etc.), pray in the body, or take a prayer walk (see Appendix C, page 89).

Group Discussion

1. What was it like to be guided to become more conscious of your breathing, to pay attention to your body and how you are caring for it, to listen to your body, to pray in your body?

Even if you felt uncomfortable or awkward, did you notice anything new through this experience?

2. Was there anything specific that your body had to say to you? Was there anything you sensed that God wanted to say to you as you became more aware of your body?

3. What aspect of honoring the body do you feel God is calling you to focus on right now? Caring for your body? Listening to your body? Praying in your body?

What would you like to try between now and the next session in response to God's invitation to you today?

Closing Prayer

Take time as a group to pray in some of the following directions:

- Thank God for the gift of life in your body. Be specific, if possible.
- If you struggle to experience life in your body as a gift, pray that God will guide you in knowing how to receive this gift.
- Pray for God's guidance in continuing to discover how you can glorify him in your body.

BETWEEN SESSIONS
Honoring God with Your Body

- **Breathe.** In your solitude times this week, begin with a few moments for breathing, settling into your body and noticing it as we did in this session.
- **Care.** This week allow your focus to be on noticing what's going on in your body and the condition of your body. How are you caring for your body? Are you eating right, drinking enough water, getting enough sleep, exercising and paying attention to fitness, going to the doctor as needed, and taking care of medical issues as they arise? What is one positive way you can care for your body this week?
- **Notice and reflect.** Record your discoveries and your thoughts about your physical condition in your journal or on the journal pages provided. Experience your desire to live well in your body and to experience your body as a gift from God. You may want to journal about your desire as well. Then listen for what God wants to say to you and how he wants to guide you in the practice of caring for your body. How are you going to arrange your life to give your body the care and attention it needs?
- **Pray in your body.** You might also want to take note of how your spiritual practices could have some connection with physical activities that you enjoy—like combining your prayer time with going for a walk.
- **Take a prayer walk.** If you have time this week, take a slow and meditative prayer walk. Notice how you experience God's presence through a greater appreciation for life in your body and through the physical, material world of which our bodies are a part. See Appendix C (page 89) for guidance in how to take a prayer walk. This practice incorporates aspects of listening to your body and praying in your body, which can be very rich and satisfying ways of connecting with God in your body.

For Further Reading

As you reflect on what you have learned in this session and practice honoring your body in between sessions, please read chapter 5 of *Sacred Rhythms.*

Reflect and Journal

Use your own journal or these journal pages to write down what you feel God said to you about honoring your body and be very specific about what you want to do in between sessions to respond to what God is saying. Then throughout the week, notice what difference your choices to honor your body are making in the quality of your life and in your relationship with God.

JOURNAL

JOURNAL

The Examen:
Bringing My Whole Self to God

Search me, O God, and know my heart; test me and know my thoughts. See if there is any wicked way in me, and lead me in the way everlasting.

— PSALM 139:23–24

THE *EXAMEN*, or the daily review, involves taking a few moments at the end of the day (or a longer period of time at the end of the week) to go back over the events of the day/ week and ask God to show us evidence of his presence (*examen of consciousness*) and ourselves in light of his presence (*examen of conscience*).

"ONE OF THE DEEPEST *longings of the human heart is to be known and loved unconditionally. We long to know that there is someone in this world who knows everything about us and loves us anyway. Beyond the surface affirmations that come through our achievements and social contacts, we long to be seen and celebrated for that which is deeply good and worthwhile in us. We long for a love that is strong enough to contain our human frailty and sinfulness. Something in us knows that such love is a transforming power.***"**

LEARN ABOUT IT
Video #1: Bringing Yourself to God (11 minutes)

As you watch the teaching segment for session five, use the following outline to record anything that stands out to you.

The *examen* is the Christian practice that opens us to the love we seek.

Psalm 139: a healthy process of self-examination involves
- vv. 1–12: *Awakening to the presence of God.* "There is no place we can go where we can fall out of the presence of God."

- vv. 13–18: *Celebrating your created goodness.* "It's hard for us to celebrate our self the way that the psalmist does."

- vv. 19–24: *Inviting God to search your heart.* "Search me, O God, and know my heart."

Examen = review of the day: "The review of the day is an opportunity for us to go back over our day with God, to do it in conversation with God."

"WHILE THE TRUTH THAT *we cannot escape God's all-seeing eye may weigh us down at times, it is finally the only remedy for our uneasiness. If we wish to hide from the penetrating gaze of holy love, it is because we know it falls on what is unholy and unloving within us. Only under God's steady gaze of love are we able to find the healing and restoration we so desperately need.***"**

— MARJORIE THOMPSON, *SOULFEAST*

Group Discussion

1. What do you see as some of the benefits of reviewing your day with God? How might this discipline help you grow?

2. How do you respond to the three moves involved in a healthy and biblical approach to self-examination — awakening the presence of God, celebrating your created goodness, and inviting God to search you and know you?

Which of these moves do you need to focus on right now?

EXPERIENCE IT
Video #2: The Examen (9 minutes)

The "Experience It" segment provides an opportunity for you to engage in a guided experience of a review of the day. Ruth Haley Barton will give specific directions in the video, so it's not necessary to follow along in your participant's guide. In fact, it is a good idea to close your book so it does not distract you. The notes below are provided as a resource and reference as you continue to practice this discipline on your own after the session.

* * *

Preparation. Spend a few moments in silence, allowing yourself to become still and aware of God's unconditional loving presence.

Review the day. The discipline commonly known as the *examen* includes the following steps:

- Look back on the events of the past twenty-four hours, asking God to guide you in seeing what he wants you to see.
- As you reflect on the events, ask God to show you where he was present with you, even though you may not have recognized it at the time.
- Ask God to show you the places where you are growing and changing. Thank him for evidence of his transforming work in your life.
- Ask God to show you places where you fell short of Christlikeness. Be careful not to succumb to shame or morbid introspection; instead, simply name your failure honestly, confess it to God, and receive his forgiveness (1 John 1:9).
- Finish by thanking God for the day and for his presence in your life.

> **OPTIONAL ACTIVITY**
> If you have more time or are in a retreat setting, this is a good occasion to spend some minutes in solitude (half an hour, ideally) to reflect more fully and possibly journal about what you discovered during this brief experience of the *examen*. You may want to reflect on your awareness of God's presence with you or take more time for self-awareness and celebration or confession.

Group Discussion

1. As you reviewed the last twenty-four hours, what did you notice about God's presence with you? Were there any surprises or revelations of God's presence where you did not expect him?

2. What did God show you about yourself—those places where you are experiencing growth and transformation *or* places where you fell short of being like Christ? What was it like to see yourself more clearly, and how was God with you in that?

3. Are there aspects of your day and even your life that you would not have noticed if you hadn't reviewed your day in this way? Describe.

4. Does the *examen* (the review of the day) seem valuable enough to incorporate it more intentionally into your life? What would that look like for you?

Closing Prayer

Take time as a group to pray in some of the following directions:

- Thank God for his presence with you and his guidance in reviewing your day.
- Thank God for evidence of his presence with you and also any insights you received about yourself in the light of God's presence.
- Ask God to help you become more aware of his presence with you in all of life and to grow in your ability to choose Christlikeness in areas where you find it most challenging.

BETWEEN SESSIONS

Practicing the Examen

Consider how you might incorporate the practice of self-examination (*examen*) during this next week. Would it work for you to practice this discipline daily by going for a walk sometime in the evening? Or would it work better for you to sit quietly for a few minutes and review your day before you go to sleep? For some it works best to take a longer period of time on the weekend to review the entire week.

You may want to reread Psalm 139 as a way of reminding yourself of God's unconditionally loving presence and to help you move through the different aspects of the *examen* — noticing God's presence, seeing yourself and your life more clearly in light of God's presence, and asking God to search your heart and reveal what you need to know.

This is a practice that incorporates all of the elements of self-examination that we have explored in this session. Once you get used to the process, you can incorporate this practice as a part of your evening or bedtime ritual. It can take as little as five minutes and, if you have time, you can incorporate some journaling about what you are noticing and learning. Some people prefer to do a daily *examen* while others prefer to do it weekly.

Preparation. Spend a few moments in silence, allowing yourself to become still and aware of God's unconditional loving presence. Use a favorite Scripture, prayer, or other spiritual reading as needed in order to settle into the assurance of God's love in the present moment. Hear God say to you, "I have loved you with an everlasting love."

Review the day. Identify the major events of the day, including your spiritual practices, meals, appointments, interactions with others, significant events at work, etc. Invite God to go with you in your search for evidence of his presence throughout your day and also in your search for self-knowledge. Reflect on each of the events as if they had been recorded on video; notice where God seemed to be loving you, speaking to you, guiding you, or showing you something new about himself. Allow God to show you evidence of his transforming work in your life and celebrate that evidence.

Give thanks. Thank God for each part of your day, for his presence with you in the midst of it, for those moments when you sensed a growing freedom from sin and a greater capacity to love God and others. If there are any unresolved issues or questions pertaining to the events of the day, express these to God as well and allow yourself to experience gratitude for God's presence with you even in places that feel dark or confusing.

Confess. Using Psalm 139:23–24 as your prayer, invite God to bring to mind attitudes, actions, or moments when you fell short of exhibiting the character of Christ or the fruit of the Spirit. As God brings different areas to mind, reflect on what it was that contributed to the situation and what might enable you to respond differently in the future.

Ask forgiveness and express your willingness to take whatever concrete steps are needed to allow Christ's character to be more fully formed in you. Be assured of God's forgiveness (1 John 1:9) and his power to continue leading you into the transformation you desire. Ask God if there is anything you need to do to make things right relative to the situation you have confessed.

Seek out spiritual friendship. Share with a spiritual friend what you are discovering about yourself, your confession, and your resolve to pursue transformation in this area.

For Further Reading
As you reflect on what you have learned in this session and seek to practice the *examen*, read chapter 5 of *Sacred Rhythms*.

Reflect and Journal
Use your journal or the journal pages provided to keep track of your "God sightings" this week and also to record and reflect upon what God is showing you about yourself in light of his presence. Don't forget to ask God to show you evidence of growth and transformation and also those places where you fell short. Remember, the purpose of the *examen* is not shame and blame but rather to give you the opportunity to take responsibility for sin and bad behavior, to confess and receive God's forgiveness, and then to ask God to help you to choose differently next time.

JOURNAL

JOURNAL

A Rule of Life: Cultivating Your Own Sacred Rhythms

Ask me not where I live or what I like to eat. . . . Ask me what I am living for and what I think is keeping me from living fully for that.

— Thomas Merton

> **A RULE OF LIFE** is a pattern of attitudes, behaviors, and practices — sacred rhythms — that we choose regularly and routinely in order to create space for God to do his transforming work in our lives.

"ONCE WE HAVE EXPERIENCED *some of the possibilities for arranging our lives around our hearts' deepest desire, the question is 'How bad do I want it? Do I want it badly enough to rearrange my life?' If the answer is yes, we can express our desire and our willingness to God directly. At the same time, it is important that we acknowledge the mystery of spiritual transformation and our powerlessness to bring it about. We need to know, really know, that spiritual transformation at this level is pure gift as we make ourselves available to God. Otherwise our rhythm of spiritual practices can become nothing more than a spiritual self-help program that is full of human effort.*"

69

intentionally

4 x 8   8:50

400 – 8:50

I want more God

LEARN ABOUT IT
Video #1: Your Own Sacred Rhythms (12 minutes)

As you watch the teaching segment for session six, use the following outline to record anything that stands out to you.

Appreciating the rhythms of life

rhythm – space / structure   *hope*

A rule of life.

arrange life. takes time and practice — discipline — Start with solitude

more time together — Be honest about my life — demands of our life — God and I her

balanced — stretch you. character. Open and available

Rule of life: rhythms that provide structure and space for our growth will be

- PERSONAL. Start with one or two disciplines you feel drawn to or that correspond to areas of need. Practice them in ways that fit your personality and the particularities of your life.

We are all together,

- REALISTIC. Take into account your current stage of life, your schedule, the demands of your family and your work, etc.

By practicing, 90 mins in the morning. sitting and resting reading scriptures

- BALANCED. Keep a balance between various disciplines—those that come easily for you and those that stretch you.

We start with our desires.

- FLEXIBLE. Hold your rhythms flexibly rather than being rigid about them.

Two questions: *Who do I want to be?* and *How do I want to live?*

How do I want to live so I can be who I want to be?

“SPIRITUAL DISCIPLINES ARE THE *main way we offer our bodies up to God as a living sacrifice. We are doing what we can do with our bodies, our minds, our hearts. God then takes this simple offering of ourselves and does with it what we cannot do, producing within us deeply ingrained habits of love and peace and joy in the Holy Spirit.***”**

— RICHARD FOSTER

Group Discussion

1. As we come to the end of this study, how are you experiencing your desire now? What does it feel like? What words seem to describe it? Is it the same or different from when we started?

2. As you think back on your experiences with the spiritual practices you have experienced in this curriculum, are there any practices that seem so compelling and important to you that you would want to arrange your life not to miss them? Describe what those are and why.

EXPERIENCE IT
Video #2: A Rule of Life (11 minutes)

Unlike the other "Experience It" segments in previous sessions, this will be a "working" session to help you begin developing your own rule of life. After you have watched the video, take some time to individually work through the directions included below. You may want to record your answers in your journal or on the blank journal pages at the end of this session. After a few minutes, proceed to the Group Discussion questions.

* * *

Begin identifying your own sacred rhythms—personal patterns, practices, experiences, and relationships that keep you open to God's transforming presence and work in your life.

- **Get in touch with what you want.** Get back in touch with the desire you were naming at the beginning of this study. Do you want it badly enough to make changes in how you are ordering your life?
- **Acknowledge your powerlessness.** Only God can do the work of transformation. Our part is to create the conditions in which spiritual transformation can take place.
- **Identify the disciplines that are life-giving for you.** Identify disciplines that energize you or seem to stretch you in some way. Look for the one(s) you feel most drawn and invited into. Do *something* before you do *everything*.
- **Think about concrete time frames.** Start by just setting aside ten minutes or half an hour daily. When you think about your day, when would be the best time for you to incorporate the disciplines you are feeling drawn to?
- **How do these disciplines work into your life?** Look at your life and think about what it would mean to actually work some of these disciplines into the time frames of your life.
- **Be realistic.** Do not set expectations for yourself that you're not going to be able to handle. Start out with one or two disciplines and capture your intention in writing. After you have written

down your plan for implementing the discipline(s) into your life, take a step back from it to make sure it is realistic.

- **Share your plan with someone else.** Share your plan with your group and/or with someone else who knows you well and who cares about you. Invite them to pray with you, and tell them that you would like them to check in with you every so often to see how your rhythms are going.

OPTIONAL ACTIVITY

If you have additional time or are using this study in a retreat setting, work further on your rule of life. Taking time "alone together" while individuals do this work is a great motivation to craft your rule of life now rather than putting it off. Also, if you have the time, consider additional group discussion for members to share their rule of life and the challenges they might face in sticking with it.

"IN THE FINAL ANALYSIS, *there is nothing I can do to transform myself into a person who loves and serves as Jesus did except to make myself available for God to do the work of transforming grace in my life.*"

— ROBERT MULHOLLAND

Group Discussion

1. What are the rhythms you sense God inviting you to establish in your life? Remember not to overcommit yourself or try to change too much all at once.

2. What do you feel are the challenges you might face as you seek to live into these new rhythms?

3. How can we pray for each other as we move forward?

Closing Prayer

Use this time of closing prayer to pray for yourselves and each other as you commit yourselves to a rule of life. Pray with special attention to the challenges that each person has shared. Do not try to offer simple answers or advice in your prayers, but instead offer that person and his or her unique challenges to God. Designate someone to close your time together with a prayer of thanksgiving and commitment as you wrap up this study together.

- Thank God for giving you the opportunity to explore practices that draw us closer to him. Thank him for the ways in which he met you during this study. Be specific.
- Pray for each individual—that they will be able to live into the plan they have put together.
- Pray for the challenges each person faces and for the discipline and ongoing resolve to order their lives around what matters most.

IN THE COMING DAYS

Developing a Rule of Life

Living into what we want in any area of our life requires some sort of intentional approach. Building a solid financial base, planning for retirement, making home improvements, advancing our career, furthering our education, losing weight, or becoming more fit—all of these require a plan if we are to make any progress in achieving what we desire.

The desire for a way of life that creates space for God's transforming work is no different. It doesn't happen by accident! But if we look closely at the way we live day to day, we may well notice that our approach to spiritual transformation is much more random and haphazard than our approach to finances, home improvements, and physical fitness! Many of us try to shove spiritual transformation into the nooks and crannies of a life that is already unmanageable, rather than being willing to arrange our life for what we say we really want.

Jesus had something to say about this. He used parables to picture a person who has searched long and hard for something very valuable and very special. In one story the prized item is a piece of land; in another it is a valuable pearl. In both stories, the merchant has been looking for this prize all his life, and when he finds it, he doesn't hesitate. He sells everything he has—he rearranges his life—so he can buy what he has been searching for.

Both the field and the pearl are metaphors for the kingdom of God— that state of being in which God is reigning in our life and his presence is shaping our reality. The kingdom of God is here now, if we are willing to arrange our life to embrace it. We all have the same choice—whether or not to arrange our lives around the practices that will nourish our souls and transform our lives.

- **Attend to your desire.** Ask: What words, phrases, and prayers seem to most consistently capture my sense of longing for God and for spiritual transformation as I'm experiencing it these days? What do I sense is most needed these days?
- **Be honest with God about the area(s) in your life right now where transformation is needed.** Acknowledge your powerless-

ness to bring it about and speak to God about your desire to make yourself available to him in a consistent way so that he can do his transforming work in you.

- **Reflect on your experiences with spiritual practices** in this study and in other experiences you have had. Invite God to show you which practices have been most life-giving to you. In particular, notice those practices in which God met you in the context of doing them. Also, notice which practices stretched you in ways you needed to be stretched and yet still seemed to result in deeper levels of connection with God and movement toward Christlikeness. Ask: Which spiritual practices and relationships seem to be most powerful in fulfilling the desires of my heart right now?
- **Based on these reflections, begin developing simple rhythms** that take into account the limits and opportunities of your life stage, your personality, and your circumstances. What are you beginning to understand about your minimum daily/weekly/monthly requirements for ongoing spiritual formation? What practices, experiences, and relationships do you want to engage in as ways of offering yourself to God steadily and consistently? Ask God for his guidance in putting together a rhythm of any of the following spiritual practices that will meet your desire for life-giving connection with him and authentic spiritual transformation.

  Solitude and silence
  Breath prayer and other kinds of prayer
  Lectio divina
  The *examen* or review of the day
  Confession
  Honoring the body
  Spiritual friendship (what you have experienced in this group)
  Another discipline
- **Get practical.** Ask: What practices will I seek to engage in on a daily basis? Weekly? Monthly? Yearly? Where will I engage in these disciplines? What time of the day/week/month/year? How will I need to adjust my schedule in order to consistently choose this rule of life? What conversations or arrangements do I need to make with those with whom I live and work?

- **Engage community.** The spiritual journey is not meant to be taken alone. Reflect on the benefits of sharing this journey into sacred rhythms with other like-minded people. What have you learned about the importance of community for the spiritual journey and how will you continue to share your journey with others in ways that are mutually beneficial?

"SPIRITUAL FRIENDSHIP IS NOT *primarily a social relationship that exists for the purpose of catching up over lunch or an occasional lunch or a golf outing.... Rather it is a relationship that is focused intentionally on our relationship with God as viewed through the lens of desire. With such a friend we share the deepest desires of our heart, so that we can support one another in arranging our lives in ways that are congruent with what our hearts want most.*"

For Further Reading
As you continue to reflect on what you have learned and work on developing your own rule of life, read chapter 9 of *Sacred Rhythms*, which contains more information and guidance regarding this important process.

Reflect and Journal
Use your own journal or this journal space to capture what it is you are committing yourself to and to ask for God's help. Then use your journal as often as you can to record how you are choosing to create space for God in your life and how you are experiencing God with you in the context of your spiritual practices.

JOURNAL

JOURNAL

Appendix A

Guide for Group Leaders

Thank you for being willing to lead and facilitate this spiritual formation experience with your small group. Here are a few suggestions to help you prepare and lead the group effectively.

CLARIFY THE PURPOSE

It is important to begin the *Sacred Rhythms* experience by clarifying the purpose of the group as described in the section titled "Welcome to *Sacred Rhythms*" (page 9). Since this study may be a bit different from other small group studies you have led, be sure to draw the group's attention to the fact that you are gathering to listen to one another's desire for God, to support one another in the spiritual practices that help us seek God, and to assist one another in paying attention to the activity of God in our everyday lives and in our spiritual practices.

Also review together the section titled "Before You Get Started ... Guidelines for Spiritual Friends" (page 11) and encourage people to agree verbally or by signing the bottom of the page that they are indeed willing to companion one another in this way. As the group leader you will need to model these values and behaviors for the group. At times, you may need to remind the group why they are together and how they should be interacting with one another. If the group digresses into mere discussion of ideas, advice-giving, problem-solving, or information-sharing, you may need to call them back to the purpose and commitments of the group. Remember that the focus is on *transformation*, not simply *information*!

PREPARE YOURSELF

The best way for you as a leader to prepare for each session is to become familiar with the video segments and the participant's guide content for that session. It will be very helpful if you are somewhat comfortable with the spiritual practice being discussed in each session and have some idea of what it involves. If you have time, it would also be highly beneficial to read the corresponding chapter (listed in "For Further Reading") in the *Sacred Rhythms* book and then practice the discipline as described in the "Between Sessions" section. Not only will this prepare you to guide your group, it will also help you to anticipate how your group may respond so you can ease their way along. Your comfort level with the practices is the best thing you can offer to your group. From time to time you might even consider sharing your experiences with the practice at the beginning of the session, just to let people know that you are a learner, that you are benefitting personally from the disciplines, and that this experience is a valuable one for you to share together.

FOLLOW THE FLOW

Begin each session (starting in session two) with a few moments of sharing how your practice of the previous discipline went. Then, as much as possible, follow the suggested flow of the participant's guide. Each session is designed to guide people *gradually* from:

- Teaching and learning from a biblical perspective (**"Learn About It"**), followed by group discussion, to
- Experiencing the discipline (**"Experience It"**), followed by another group discussion, to
- Practicing the discipline and reflecting on it afterward (**"Between Sessions"/"In the Coming Days"**).

Although the guided experiences may feel uncomfortable at first, you will serve the group well by making sure that you don't just talk about the disciplines, but actually experience them together. Closing your time with prayer that celebrates what God is doing in each person's life and seeks God's help for the week to come is an important way of "gathering up" all that has been shared and entrusting it to God. *All of the components taken together are the best way for this type of learning to take place.*

OTHER FORMATS

The materials in the *Sacred Rhythms* video study are designed to be used in six sessions. However, the material can be adapted to various learning environments. If you find that one group time is not long enough to fully engage all the components contained in each session, feel free to adapt the material to suit your needs. Here are some suggestions.

Twelve Sessions

One option is to extend your time together by meeting twice for each session (twelve meetings instead of six). The first meeting for each session will allow you sufficient time to begin by discussing your practice from the previous week, sharing with the group how your individual time of learning between sessions went, and what you learned from that time. Then, the group can take time to listen to the teaching and discuss the new discipline for that week (the "Learn About It" segment followed by discussion). Group members can then do some additional reading and study during the week (exploring the Scripture passages cited in that session and reading the corresponding chapter in the book *Sacred Rhythms*), and at the second meeting the group can go through the guided experience together and have ample time for the group discussion that follows. This allows even more time to share with one another how you are planning to incorporate that practice between sessions. This format also will enable you to do the "Optional Activity," which provides guidance for practicing the discipline *during* your group time.

Weekend Retreat or Seminar

Another possibility is to use this curriculum for a weekend seminar or retreat for a larger group. Some may even want to lead an entire congregation through a study of these spiritual practices starting in the evening on the first day and going through noon on the third day. (i.e., Thursday night–Saturday noon, Friday night–Sunday noon, etc.). The seminar or retreat format could include all six sessions, with time built in for additional solitude and personal experience with the discipline as indicated in the "Optional Activity."

CONCLUDING THOUGHTS

In the end, the most important thing you can do as a group leader is to be faithful to your own exploration of the spiritual practices so that you are able to share honestly and offer perspective that comes from personal experience. Be sure to share both your successes *and* struggles as a fellow traveler on the journey of spiritual transformation. Remember that everyone's experiences will be different and that responses to them will vary. Don't let that throw you. *God's job* is to guide people in their spiritual journeys and to bring about the needed transformation in their lives. *Your job* as a group leader is to help maintain a safe, nonjudgmental environment in which a variety of experiences can be shared, questions can be raised, and evidence of God's presence and activity can be celebrated.

ADDITIONAL RESOURCES ONLINE

For additional resources, articles, and supplemental materials that leaders can use for retreats or for leading small group discussions, please visit *www.thetransformingcenter.org* and look for the *Sacred Rhythms* resource page.

Appendix B

"There Is Something I Wanted to Tell You"

The following prayer, adapted from Ted Loder's *Guerrillas of Grace* (Minneapolis: Augsburg, 1981) and used by permission, is referred to in session two of this curriculum.

> Holy One,
> there is something I wanted to tell you,
> but there have been errands to run,
>   bills to pay,
>   arrangements to make,
>   meetings to attend,
>   friends to entertain,
>   washing to do . . .
> and I forget what it is I wanted to say to you,
>   and mostly I forget what I'm about,
>   or why.
> O God,
> don't forget me, please,
> for the sake of Jesus Christ.
>
> Eternal One,
> there is something I wanted to tell you,
> but my mind races with worrying and watching,
>   with weighing and planning,
>   with rutted slights and pothole grievances,
>   with leaky dreams I keep trying to plug up;

and my attention is preoccupied
  with loneliness,
    with doubt,
      and with things I covet;
and I forget what it is I wanted to say to you,
  and how to say it honestly
    or how to do much of anything.
O God,
don't forget me please,
for the sake of Jesus Christ.

Almighty One,
there is something I wanted to tell you
but I stumble along the edge of a nameless rage,
haunted by a hundred floating fears and ...
I forget what the real question is that I wanted to ask,
  and I forget to listen anyway
    because you seem unreal and far away,
and I forget what it is I have forgotten.
O God,
don't forget me please,
for the sake of Jesus Christ.

O Father in heaven,
perhaps you've already heard what I wanted to tell you.
What I wanted to ask is
  forgive me,
    heal me,
      increase my courage, please.
Renew in me a little of love and faith,
  and a sense of confidence,
    and a vision of what it might mean
      to live as though you were real,
        and I mattered,
          and everyone was sister and brother.
What I wanted to ask in my blundering way is

don't give up on me,
don't become too sad about me,
but laugh with me
and try again with me,
and I will with you, too.
What I wanted to ask is
for peace enough to want and work for more,
for joy enough to share,
and for awareness that is keen enough
to sense your presence
here,
now,
there,
then,
always.

APPENDIX C

Taking a Prayer Walk

Just a closer walk with Thee,
Grant it, Jesus, is my plea.
Daily walking close to Thee,
Let it be, dear Lord,
Let it be.

—AN OLD GOSPEL HYMN

Walking with God is a much-used metaphor for the life of faith—a life characterized by intimacy with God. Enoch, Noah, and David were all described as those who walked with God and pleased God with their very lives. In Scripture, walking with someone implies a level of agreement and mutual influence. How can two *walk* together unless they are agreed? asks the prophet Amos (Amos 3:3). The psalmist (Psalm 1:1) says that we are blessed when we do not *walk* in the way of sinners—in other words, when we do not allow ourselves to be influenced by those who are cynical about God and God's ways. And one of the clearest and most succinct descriptions of what God wants from us is to do justice, to love kindness, and to *walk* humbly with our God (Micah 6:8).

A prayer walk is just that—a walk that is taken for the purpose of being with God. Although we know that God is always present with us whenever and wherever we walk, a prayer walk or a walking meditation is taken with a greater level of intentionality about being awake to and aware of God's presence with us as we walk. A prayer walk is a spiritual discipline, in that we consciously invite God to go with us, ask him to help us experience fully the extraordinary gift of being in our bodies, and (when we are able to take our walk outdoors) invite him to reveal something of himself through nature. *The heavens declare the greatness of the Lord*, Scripture tells us in numerous places. On a prayer walk we seek to be alert to the ways in which nature reveals God to us on this day, in this particular moment of our lives.

In light of the significance that Scripture places on this idea of walking with another person, it can be exciting (or at least fill us with a quiet sense of anticipation) to think about taking a walk that is more intentionally oriented toward opening to the presence of God, enjoying the intimacy of that relationship, looking at things together, and allowing ourselves to be influenced by him as we walk. Be sure to schedule your walk so that you do not have to worry about time. If possible, leave your watch at home.

A SIMPLE PROCESS

Following are a few suggestions for being open and receptive to God's presence in the context of your walk. Don't take this guide with you. Instead, read it ahead of time for ideas, but then let God and your own body guide you as you take your walk.

1. **Be in your body.** Begin by simply standing and being aware of your posture, your breathing, and your balance. Notice how your weight is being transferred through the soles of your feet and onto the earth. Be aware of all the subtle movements that keep you balanced and upright and how we take this ability for granted. Be aware of whether or not you are slouching; pull your shoulders back so that you are more "centered" and open in your body and so that your chest can be more expansive to allow for deeper breathing.

2. **Breathe.** Take several deep breaths as a way of getting in touch with your body in God's presence. Allow yourself to become more conscious of the fact that God gives you every breath you take and with each breath he is affirming your life and presence on this earth. As you breathe, notice any place of tension or tightness in your body—clenched fists, a tight jaw, tension in your shoulders. Consciously breathe into that place and allow your breathing to release the tension as much as possible.

3. **Acknowledge God's presence and invite him to walk with you.** Before you begin your actual walk, allow yourself to experience excitement, a sense of anticipation, or just a feeling of peace at being one who "walks with God" on this day. If you have any doubt or cynicism about what this experience might be like, express that too, but still—be sure to offer an invitation to God to speak to you and to show you things about himself that you need to know. If you have a question you are wrestling with these days, feel free to take the question with you—not to work on it intellectually to find an answer, but in the spirit of saying to God as you might say to a friend, "Could we go for a walk together? I have something I want to talk to you about."

4. **Walk.** As you begin, walk at a fairly slow but normal walking pace and in a normal manner. One of the main differences between a prayer walk and a normal walk is that on a prayer walk, we are not trying to get somewhere and there is no agenda except to be fully present in this moment/step and in the next and the next and the next.

5. **Notice everything—inside and out.** Notice what it is like to walk with an unhurried pace—your body fully upright and planted in this step rather that straining forward as you usually do, rushing from one place to the next. Notice the sensations in your body—the rhythm and pattern of your footfalls, the significance of your ankles in the process of walking, the strength of your legs, the swaying of your hips, your belly as the core or center of your body (rather than your head). Notice how your clothing feels, whether it is comfortable or uncomfortable, whether it contributes to your ability to walk with comfort and strength or whether it hinders you in any way. Notice your thoughts, feelings, and emotions without getting all wrapped up in them or judging them. Just notice them with curiosity and interest and then let them pass through you. If they are significant, they will come back.

6. **Feel free to just walk quietly and receptively** *or* to talk to God as you walk.

7. **Stop when something catches your eye or draws you in. Do not be afraid to leave the beaten path.** Since you have invited God to guide this walk, trust what happens on it. If you see something in nature that is beautiful or interesting or curious, stop and allow yourself to be drawn into that and fully present to it. Stay as long as you like. *You have no place else to go that is more important.* Let God speak to you in and through it or just enjoy the beauty of it and the freedom of not having to rush on.

8. **Conclude your walk as you began it—by being in your body and thanking God for his presence with you.** As you arrive back at the place you began, give yourself a few moments to be grateful for the amount of health and strength you have in your body that enabled you to take this walk. Thank God for the gift of life in a body. And thank God for the gift of living *your* life in a body in his loving and life-affirming presence. You might also want to note anything you learned about walking with God as a result of taking this prayer walk.

Also available from InterVarsity Press

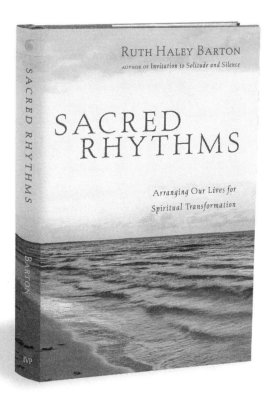

ISBN 978-0-8308-3333-7
HARDCOVER, 192 PAGES

Discounts Available on Bulk Orders

To order, please visit www.ivpress.com/sacredrhythms
or call 1-800-843-9487.

Use the following coupon code when ordering: 506-286.
(U. S. orders only)

Share Your Thoughts

With the Author: Your comments will be forwarded to the author when you send them to *zauthor@zondervan.com*.

With Zondervan: Submit your review of this book by writing to *zreview@zondervan.com*.

Free Online Resources at

www.zondervan.com

Zondervan AuthorTracker: Be notified whenever your favorite authors publish new books, go on tour, or post an update about what's happening in their lives at www.zondervan.com/authortracker.

Daily Bible Verses and Devotions: Enrich your life with daily Bible verses or devotions that help you start every morning focused on God. Visit www.zondervan.com/newsletters.

Free Email Publications: Sign up for newsletters on Christian living, academic resources, church ministry, fiction, children's resources, and more. Visit www.zondervan.com/newsletters.

Zondervan Bible Search: Find and compare Bible passages in a variety of translations at www.zondervanbiblesearch.com.

Other Benefits: Register yourself to receive online benefits like coupons and special offers, or to participate in research.

ZONDERVAN®

ZONDERVAN.com/
AUTHORTRACKER
follow your favorite authors